Master Math

MeaSuRe UP

Length, mass, capacity, time, and money

ANJANA CHATTERJEE   ILLUSTRATED BY JO SAMWAYS

CONSULTATION BY
RUTH BULL, BSc (HONS), PGCE, MA (ED)

Quarto is the authority on a wide range of topics.

Quarto educates, entertains and enriches the lives of our readers—enthusiasts and lovers of hands-on living.

www.quartoknows.com

Author: Anjana Chatterjee
Consultant: Ruth Bull, BSc (HONS), PGCE, MA (ED)
Designers: emojo design and Victoria Kimonidou
Illustrator: Jo Samways
Editors: Claire Watts and Ellie Brough

© 2018 Quarto Publishing plc
First Published in 2018 by The Quarto Library,
an imprint of The Quarto Group.
6 Orchard Road, Suite 100
Lake Forest, CA 92630
T: +1 949 380 7510
F: +1 949 380 7575
www.QuartoKnows.com

Distributed in the United States and Canada by
Lerner Publisher Services
241 First Avenue North
Minneapolis, MN 55401 U.S.A.
www.lernerbooks.com

A CIP record for this book is available at the Library of Congress.

ISBN 978 1 68297 321 9

9 8 7 6 5 4 3 2 1

Manufactured in DongGuan, China TL102017

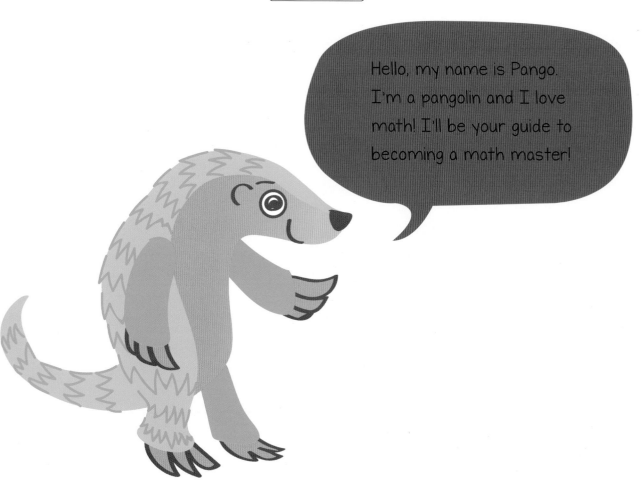

Hello, my name is Pango. I'm a pangolin and I love math! I'll be your guide to becoming a math master!

CONTENTS

HOW TO USE THE BOOKS IN THIS SERIES

The four books in Year 1 of the Master Math series focus on the main strands of the curriculum but using the leading Singapore math approach. This method involves teaching children to think and explain mathematically, with an emphasis on problem solving, focusing on the following three-step approach:

1 Concrete

Children engage in hands-on learning activities using concrete objects such as counters, cubes, dice, paper clips, or buttons. For example, children might add 4 cubes and 3 cubes together.

2 Pictorial

Children draw pictorial representations of mathematical concepts. For example, children might draw a number bond diagram showing that 3 and 4 together make 7.

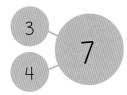

3 Abstract

Children can then move on to solving mathematical problems in an abstract way by using numbers and symbols. Once children understand that 3 and 4 make 7 when they are added together, they can use the abstract method to record it.

$$3 + 4 = 7$$

Each unit of the book begins with a question or statement that encourages children to begin thinking about a new mathematical concept. This is followed by visual explanations and hands-on activities that lead children to a deep conceptual understanding. Children should repeat and vary the activities, and be encouraged to revisit earlier sections to seek clarification and to deepen their understanding. You will find extension activities and further instruction in the Parent and Teacher Guidance sections.

When we talk about how long and short things are, we are talking about **length**.

Look at the pictures.

Can you find a long pencil and a short pencil?

The green pencil is **long**.
The red pencil is **short**.

The yellow scarf is long.
The orange scarf is short.

COMPARE THE LENGTHS

Compare the length of some things from your pencil case.
Line up a pencil and an eraser so they have the same starting point.

ends lined up →

Which object is long?
Which object is short?

The pencil is **longer** than the rubber.
The eraser is **shorter** than the pencil.

PARENT AND TEACHER GUIDANCE
● Remind children that in order to compare lengths they need to line up one end of the objects they are comparing.

Now line up 3 things.

The pencil is **longest**.
The eraser is **shortest**.

VOCABULARY: length, long, short, compare, longer, shorter, longest, shortest

SHORT AND TALL

When we talk about how short or **tall**
something is, we are talking about **height**.

The cereal box is tall.
The juice carton is short.

Let's compare these 3 bears.
The blue bear is **taller** than the green bear.
The brown bear is shorter than the green bear.
Which bear is **tallest**?
Which bear is shortest?

HOW LONG?

Let's **measure** with paper clips.

The paintbrush is the same length as 8 paper clips.
We can say that the paintbrush is 8 paper clips long.

TRY THIS:
Measure some more objects.
How many teaspoons long is your book?
How many crayons high is the table?

PARENT AND TEACHER GUIDANCE
● Before children move on to measure
using standard measures, they need lots
of practice in using non-standard units,
such as paper clips, toy cars, or crayons.

VOCABULARY: tall, height, taller, tallest, measure

MEASURING AND COMPARING

We can measure length and height in lots of different ways.
We call the thing we're using to measure the **unit** of measurement.

handspans

feet

paces

paperclips

bricks

pencils

DIFFERENT OBJECTS, SAME UNIT

Look at the paintbrushes
Which paintbrush is longer?
How do you know?

Measure some different objects with the same unit.
Say which is longer and which is shorter.

SAME OBJECT, DIFFERENT UNITS

Look at the cereal box.
How many juice cartons high is the cereal box?
How many cans high is the cereal box?

Measure an object with two or more different units.
Why do you think the number of units is different
each time?

VOCABULARY: unit

MEASURING IN INCHES

Let's find out how to measure using a **ruler**.
Look at the marks on this ruler.
Each mark shows an **inch**.

An inch is always the same length on any ruler.

An inch is a unit of measurement.
We can use this ruler to measure things in inches.
We use a ruler to measure things **accurately**.

TRY THIS:

Line a crayon up with the line marked 0 on the ruler.
Find the mark nearest to the other end of the crayon.
That shows you how long the crayon is in inches.
This crayon is 4 inches long.

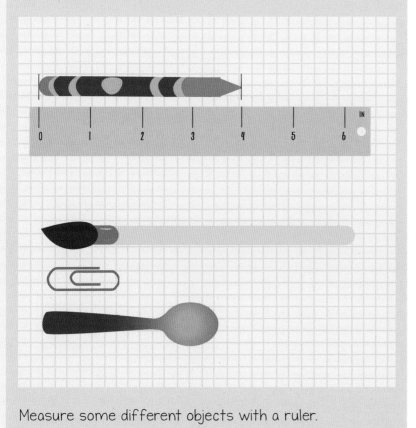

Measure some different objects with a ruler.

PARENT AND TEACHER GUIDANCE

- As children measure different objects with the same unit, they will see that different-sized objects give different measurements. When they measure the same object with different units, they will see that they will need different numbers of units.

- Children are not expected to use standard measures in the first years of school. As they begin to learn, they will be taught both US customary units (inches and feet) as well as metric units (centimetres and metres).

VOCABULARY: ruler, inch, accurate

MEASURING IN YARDS

When we measure things that are very
long or very tall we use a different unit.
We use a longer unit called a **yard**.

A yard is the same
as 36 inches.

We can use a **yard stick** to measure yards.
Each small mark on the yard stick is one inch.

We can also measure in yards with a **measuring tape**.
Can you see the inch marks?

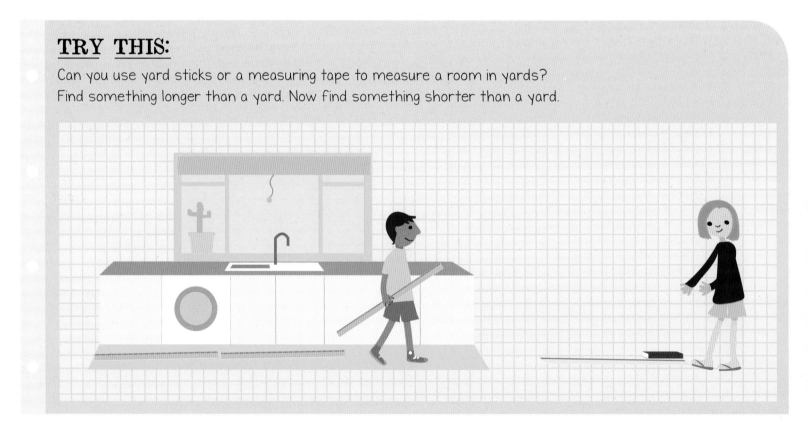

TRY THIS:

Can you use yard sticks or a measuring tape to measure a room in yards?
Find something longer than a yard. Now find something shorter than a yard.

PARENT AND TEACHER GUIDANCE

- At this stage children will be looking at whole yards and inches only.
  Real-world measuring may raise questions about this. Use language such as
  "a bit more than," "a bit less than," "and a bit," "nearly," "almost," or "over".

VOCABULARY: yard, yard stick, measuring tape

TIME TO PRACTICE!

Let's do some measuring.

How many inches long is each object?
Look at the ruler beneath each object
to find the object's length.

Which is longer, the eraser or the toy car?
Which of the 3 objects is the longest?
Which object is the shortest?

Use a ruler to find an object that
is longer than the toothbrush.
Now find something that is shorter
than the eraser.

TRY THIS:

How long is this table?
Use a yard stick to find an object that is longer
than the table. Now find something that is shorter
than the table.

PARENT AND TEACHER GUIDANCE

- Children need plenty of practice with measuring length before tackling height.

- Children could use string cut into yard lengths for measuring if you do not have yard sticks.

- Discuss the difference between length, width, and height with children.

Now try measuring how high a table is.

UNIT 2 HEAVY AND LIGHT

When we talk about how **heavy** or **light** something
is, we are talking about **weight** or **mass**.

Look at the book and the pencil.

The book is heavy.
The pencil is light.

The book is **heavier** than the pencil.
The pencil is **lighter** than the book.

Pick up this book.
Do you think it's heavy?

COMPARING WEIGHT

Find two objects you can hold in your hands.

Which one is heavier?
Which one is lighter?

Choose some other objects.
Here are some things you could try.
What is the **heaviest** object you have found?
What is the **lightest** object?

PARENT AND TEACHER GUIDANCE

- At this stage, the words "mass" and "weight" may be used interchangeably.

- Prompt children to discover that they will have to compare each object with
  several others to discover the heaviest and the lightest.

VOCABULARY: heavy, light, weight, mass, heavier, lighter, heaviest, lightest

THINK ABOUT IT

Let's look at some different objects and compare how heavy they are.

Look at the pictures.

Which object is heavy?
Which object is light?

You can't hold all these objects in your hands, so you will have to think hard!

car

bicycle

strawberry

watermelon

baby

grown-up

PARENT AND TEACHER GUIDANCE

● Mass is a more complex measure for children than length because it cannot be visualized and because direct comparison of the mass of objects is imprecise unless a balance scale is used.

● Use household objects or toys to demonstrate to children that objects are not always heavier just because they are bigger.

MEASURING WEIGHT

We can use a **balance scale** to compare the weight of objects.

This is a balance scale.

What happens to the balance scale when we put a pencil and a juice carton in the pans?

The juice carton has gone down.
That shows that it is heavier than the pencil.

The pencil has gone up.
That shows that it is lighter than the juice carton.

BALANCED BALANCE

Look at this balance scale. What do you notice?

The pans on each side are at the same level.
The pans are balanced.

When the pans are balanced, the mass of the objects in each pan is the same.
So we know the marker has the same mass as 6 cubes.
The marker **weighs** the same as 6 cubes.

Try finding the mass of some other objects using cubes and a balance scale.
Try using different objects to measure mass with.

marbles   paper clips   pasta shells

COMPARING MASS

Let's practice comparing the mass of objects.

How many cubes does the box of crayons weigh?
Do you think it is lighter or heavier than a ruler?
How could you check?

You could compare the ruler and the crayons
on the balance scale.

You could compare both objects with cubes.
The crayons weigh 5 cubes.
The ruler weighs 1 cube.
So the crayons weigh more than the ruler.
The crayons are heavier than the ruler.

OUNCES AND POUNDS

When we are measuring mass, the units
we use are called **ounces** and **pounds**.

You can use weights like these on one side
of the balance scale to measure mass.

4 oz

This apple weighs 4 ounces.
Use ounce weights to weigh an apple.
Can you find something heavier than the apple?
Can you find something lighter?

PARENT AND TEACHER GUIDANCE

- Encourage children to estimate before they compare mass. Ask questions such as: "Which do you think is heavier: the big, empty bottle or the small, full bottle?"

- Point out to children that food packaging usually shows the mass of the contents in ounces. Can they look at different packages and say which is heavier?

- Show children different types of weighing scales and ask them to figure out how they can use the scale to measure mass.

VOCABULARY: ounces, pounds

Let's look at how much space there is inside things.

Look at this pitcher.
How would you describe it?

This pitcher is **empty**.
It has nothing inside it.

Look around you for some objects that have space inside them, such as boxes, cups and jugs.

Look at this pitcher.
How would you describe it?

This pitcher is **full**.
This pitcher has juice inside it.
It is full of juice.

Look at this pitcher.
How would you describe it?

This pitcher is **half full**.
This pitcher has some juice inside it.
It has less juice than the full pitcher.
It has more juice than the empty pitcher.

PARENT AND TEACHER GUIDANCE

- Show children two bottles, one full of water and one empty. Ask, "What's the difference between these bottles?"

- Give children empty cups and a bottle of water. Ask them to show you a full cup, an empty cup, a cup that's half full, and two cups that have more and less water in them.

VOCABULARY: empty, full, half full

WHICH HOLDS MOST?

Let's look at how much water different bottles can **hold**.

1 Look at the bottles. Which bottle do you think will hold the most? Why? Which bottle do you think will hold the least? Why?

2 Take one of your empty bottles and place the funnel in the top.

3 Fill the cup with water and pour it into the bottle. Pour in more cups of water until the bottle is full. Carefully count how many cups of water you use to fill the bottle.

YOU WILL NEED:

- some bottles in different sizes
- a funnel
- a cup
- a marker

4 Write the number of cups on the bottle with the marker.

5 Do this with the other bottles. Can you put them in order from the bottle that holds the most to the bottle that holds the least?

You can play this game with lots of **containers**. Try milk jugs and yogurt cups.

PARENT AND TEACHER GUIDANCE

- Capacity is an abstract concept, so children need a lot of guidance. Use different sized cups to ask questions such as, "Which cup do you think holds most?" "Which cup holds least?"

VOCABULARY: hold, container

DIFFERENT CONTAINERS

We use containers such as pitchers, cups, mugs, bottles, and buckets to hold liquids like water, milk, and juice.

Here are some different containers.

Can you think of some more types of containers?

The bucket holds enough water to fill 9 glasses.

The pitcher holds enough juice to fill 4 glasses.

TRY THIS:

Look at these bottles.

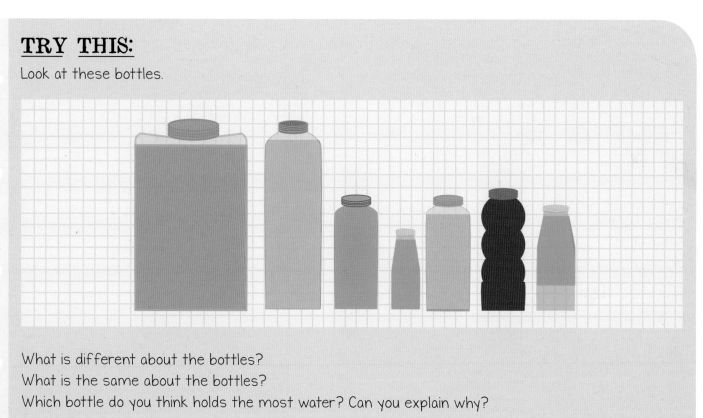

What is different about the bottles?
What is the same about the bottles?
Which bottle do you think holds the most water? Can you explain why?

THINK ABOUT IT

Let's think about how much things contain.

Look at the milk jug.
One jug can fill 5 glasses with milk.

How many glasses do you think 2 jugs can fill?
2 jugs can fill 10 glasses.

How many glasses do you think 3 milk jugs can fill?

HOW MUCH DOES IT HOLD?

The amount a container can hold is called its **capacity**. Which bottle holds more paint?

The big bottle of paint can fill 8 paint pots.
The big bottle has the same capacity as 8 paint pots.

The small bottle of paint can fill 4 paint pots. The small bottle has the same capacity as 4 paint pots.

The big bottle holds more paint than the small bottle.
The small bottle holds less paint than the big bottle.

PARENT AND TEACHER GUIDANCE
- At this stage, you may find the words "capacity" and "volume" used interchangeably. Capacity refers to the amount of space inside something. Volume is the amount of space something takes up.

VOCABULARY: capacity

When we talk about when things happen or how long they take, we are talking about **time**.

The **first** thing I do every morning is eat my breakfast.

When you get out of bed, it is usually light outside. It is the **morning**.

It's breakfast time. What will you do **next**? You might go to school.

Soon it's **night**. The sky is dark and you might see the moon or stars. It's bedtime.

Later, you will have lunch. **After** lunch, it is the **afternoon**. You might play.

Later on, it starts to get dark. It's time for a snack or dinner. It's the **evening**.

PARENT AND TEACHER GUIDANCE
• Talk to children regularly about things they have done, things they do regularly, and things they are going to do. Prompt them to use time vocabulary.

VOCABULARY: time, first, morning, next, later, after, afternoon, evening, soon, night

WHAT HAPPENED?

Let's look at how things happen in order.

These pictures are in the wrong order.

What happened first?
What happened next?
What happened **last**?

TALK ABOUT IT

Talk about your day with your friend.

Here are some time words you can use: first, next, **then**, after, **before**

What did you do after breakfast?
When did you brush your teeth?
What was the first thing you did?
Did you get up in the morning, the afternoon, or the evening?
What meal do you eat in the evening?
What did you do before lunch?

VOCABULARY: last, then, before

DAYS, WEEKS, MONTHS, AND YEARS

We measure time in **days**, **weeks**, **months**, and **years**.

Every morning when you wake up a new day starts.
There are 7 days in a week.

| Monday | Tuesday | Wednesday | Thursday | Friday | Saturday | Sunday |

The days of the week always come in this order.
After Sunday, you start again with Monday.

DAYS OF THE WEEK

Let's make a circle to show the order
of the days of the week.

YOU WILL NEED:

- sticky notes
- a long strip of paper
- paper clips

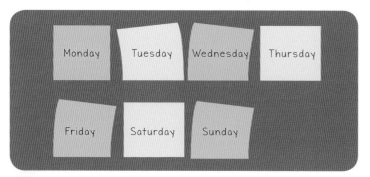

1   Write the days of the week on sticky
    notes. Stick the notes in order along
    a long strip of paper.

2   Using two paper clips, join the ends of
    the strip of paper together with the
    words on the outside.

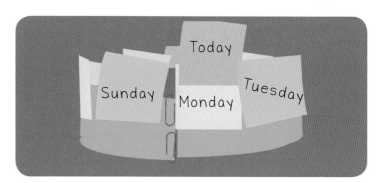

3   What day is it **today**? Turn the pad of
    sticky notes so that the sticky strip is at
    the bottom. Write the word "today" and
    stick it at the top of today's name.

4   We call the day before today **yesterday**.
    What day was it yesterday? Add a sticky
    note to mark yesterday.

5   We call the day after today **tomorrow**.
    Add a sticky note to tomorrow.

VOCABULARY: day, week, month, year, today, yesterday, tomorrow

MONTHS OF THE YEAR

Let's look at the months of the year.

This is a **calendar**.

This calendar shows the month of February.
There are 12 months in a year.
Can you see the names of the days of the week on the calendar?

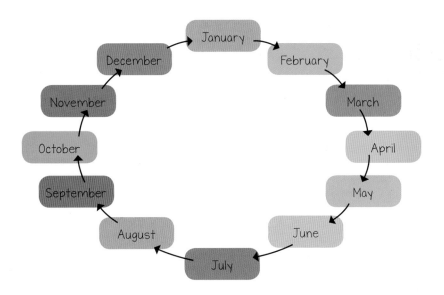

FEBRUARY

Sunday	Monday	Tuesday	Wednesday	Thursday	Friday	Saturday
1	2	3	4	5	6	7
8	9	10	11	12	13	14
15	16	17	18	19	20	21
22	23	24	25	26	27	28

February usually has only 28 days.
Most of the months are 30 or 31 days long.

Which month comes after February?
Which month comes before July?
Which month comes after December?

January · February · March · April · May · June · July · August · September · October · November · December

BIRTHDAYS

Everyone has a birthday once a year.
It's a celebration of the day they were born.

This boy is 6 years old.
He is celebrating his 6th birthday.
How many years old are you?

Do you know when your birthday is?

VOCABULARY: calendar

CLOCK TIME

We now know how to measure time in months, weeks, and days. We use a **clock** to measure smaller bits of time. There are lots of different types of clocks.

Look around your home and see how many different clocks you can find.

MINUTES AND HOURS

Clocks measure **minutes** and **hours**.

On this clock, the small **hand** points to the hours.
The big hand points to the minutes.

On this clock, the number on the left shows the hours.
The number on the right shows the minutes.

TRY THIS:

Watch the hands on a clock as they move.
Which hand moves faster?

The minute hand goes faster than the hour hand. It takes one hour for the minute hand to go all the way around once. In one hour, the hour hand only moves from one number to the next one.

VOCABULARY: clock, minute, hour, hand

TELLING THE TIME

Let's find out how to read the time on a clock.

1 Look at the minute hand of the clock.
When the minute hand points straight up,
it is the beginning of a new hour.
The time is something **o'clock**.

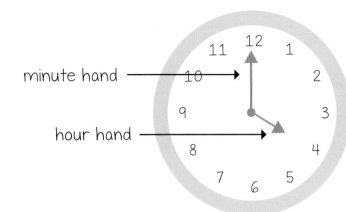

2 The hour hand points to the hours. The
hour hand on this clock is pointing to the 4.

3 The time is 4 o'clock.

1 On this clock, first look at the number on
the left. The left number tells us the hours.

2 The right number shows the minutes.
Two zeroes mean that no minutes have passed.
It is something o'clock.

3 The time is 11 o'clock.

WHAT CAN YOU DO?

Some clocks have another hand that measures
smaller units of time called **seconds**.
The second hand moves very fast.

What can you do in a second?
What can you do in a minute?
What can you do in an hour?
Ask an adult to help you find out the answers.

VOCABULARY: o'clock, second

WHAT TIME IS IT?

Read the time on the clocks.

Pippa is going to bed.
What time is it?

Pippa is playing outside.
What time is it?

It's time for breakfast.
What time is it?

 8:00

It's time for a snack.
What time is it?

10:00

TRY THIS:
Use a toy clock or draw a clock face to show these times.

School starts at 9 o'clock.   I go to bed at 8 o'clock.

What time do you go to bed?

PARENT AND TEACHER GUIDANCE
• Give children plenty of opportunities to recognize times and make them by drawing or using a geared clock.

HALF PAST

Let's think about a different time that a clock can show.

1. Pretend that your arm is a minute hand.
   Stand with your arm straight up.
   It's something o'clock.

2. Move your arm in a big circle the way the minute hand moves. When it's straight up again, a whole hour has passed.

3. Start with your arm straight up again.
   Move your arm halfway around the circle.
   Where is it pointing now?

4. When the minute hand on a clock has gone halfway around, it points straight down.
   The hour hand has moved too.
   It's halfway between the 3 and the 4.
   The time is **half past** 3.

5. On this clock, half past 3 looks like this.
   The number 30 shows that the time is 30 minutes after 3 o'clock.

TRY THIS:
Can you read the time on these clocks?

VOCABULARY: half past

We use **money** to **buy** things.
Money is made up of different **coins** and **bills**.
Each coin and bill has a **value**.

Here are the coins we use to buy things.
The front and the back of the coins look different.

Can you find any coins with jagged edges?

← penny
1 cent

← nickel
5 cents

← dime
10 cents

← quarter
25 cents

We sometimes write cents like this: ¢

Do you have a money box where you collect coins?
Open it and see how the coins look and feel.
What shape are the coins?
What color are they?
Can you see any numbers on the coins?
Can you see any words?

PARENT AND TEACHER GUIDANCE

● Most American coins have no numbers on them and the words are written in capitals which can be difficult for young children to read. Point out the number names to children, but be aware that at this stage, they will distinguish the coins by shape and color rather than the number.

● Give children opportunities to handle coins and bills.

26 **VOCABULARY:** money, buy, coin, bill, value, penny, nickel, dime, quarter, dollar

HOW MUCH ARE COINS WORTH?

Each coin has a different value.
The value tells you how much the coin is **worth**.

The number on a coin tells you its value.

This coin is worth one cent.

This coin is worth five cents.

So one nickel is worth the same as five pennies.

 =   (and more)

Can you figure out how many pennies are the same as all these coins? Draw around some coins to show your answers.

PARENT AND TEACHER GUIDANCE

- Children may notice that sometimes you pay using a card rather than with coins and bills. Explain that you keep most of your money in the bank. When you use a card, it sends a message to your bank, asking them to pay an amount of money to the seller's bank account.

DOLLARS

For greater values, we use paper money called bills. 100 cents make one dollar.

This is a dollar bill.
We can write dollar like this: **$**

A $1 bill is worth the same as four quarters.

 =

Can you see how many dollars each of these bills is worth?

VOCABULARY: worth

Remember that coins have different values. Look carefully at the number written in words or digits on each coin.

This apple costs 6 cents.

I can buy it with these coins.   nickel + penny = 6 cents

This orange costs 11 cents.
Which coins can I use to buy it?
Can you write an addition sentence to show this?

This watermelon costs 35 cents.
Which coins can I use to buy it?
Can you write an addition sentence to show this?

TRY THIS:

Add up the coins below and say which of these things you could buy with them.

12¢   9¢

15¢   26¢

Write addition sentences to show how you added the amounts.

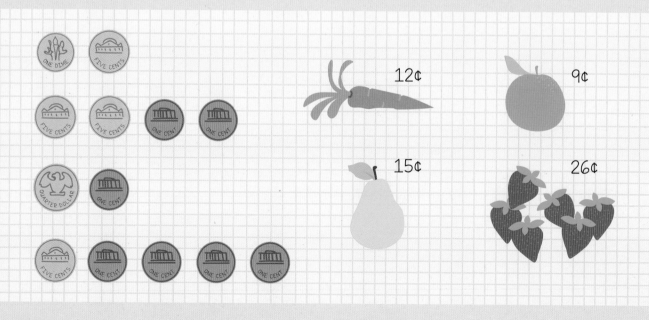

28

MAKE THE RIGHT AMOUNT

Use play money to make these amounts.

17¢   21¢   30¢   50¢

MORE OR LESS

Look at the prices of the items.

Which object costs more?
Write an addition sentence to show how
you could make each amount with coins.

17¢   21¢

Which object costs less?
Write an addition sentence to show how
you could make each amount with coins.

21¢   30¢

How much do 3 notebooks cost?
Can you show this amount with coins?

50¢   50¢   50¢

Which object costs most?
Which object costs least?

PARENT AND TEACHER GUIDANCE

- Children can use play money for these
  activities, or they can make play coins by
  drawing around real money onto stiff
  paper and cutting out the shapes.

ADDING WITH MONEY

Let's look at different ways to make amounts with coins.

These coins make 11 cents.

dime + penny = 11 cents

These coins also make 11 cents.

nickel + nickel + penny = 11 cents

Can you find any more ways to make 11 cents?

We can make 27 cents with coins like this.

quarter + penny + penny = 27 cents

Here's another way to make 27 cents.

nickel + nickel + nickel + nickel + nickel
+ penny + penny = 27 cents

And here's another way!

dime + dime + nickel + penny
+ penny = 27 cents

Can you find some more ways to make 27 cents?

If you can't read the words on the coins, ask a grown-up to help you.

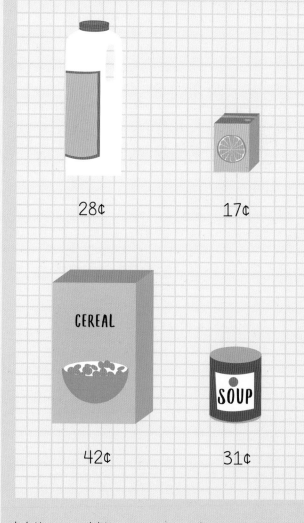

TRY THIS:

Try making each of these amounts with coins in two different ways.

28¢

17¢

CEREAL

42¢

SOUP

31¢

Write an addition sentence for each one to show your answers.

WHICH IS MORE?

Look at these groups of coins.

Which group is worth more? Add up the values of the coins to find out.

IS IT ENOUGH?

When we buy something, we have to give enough money.

Sometimes we give the **exact** amount.
The cookie costs 16 cents.
The coins are worth 16 cents.

 16¢

If we don't have the right coins to make the
exact amount, we can give more money.
The donut costs 18 cents.
The coin is worth 25 cents.
25 cents is more than 18 cents.

 18¢

The store will give us some other coins back as **change**.

Say if these amounts of money are enough to buy each thing.
Remember, you can pay the exact amount or you can pay more.

 36¢

 14¢

VOCABULARY: exact, change

TOOLS FOR SUCCESS

Most of the math activities in the book can be carried out using everyday items, but the following mathematical tools are used in this book and you may find them useful.

Ruler

6-inch or 12-inch rulers, marked with inches only, can be used to introduce children to the concept of measuring using a scale. Alternatively, you could use a metric ruler marked with s only. You should remind children how to position the ruler so that the object being measured lines up with the 0 on the ruler.

Measuring tape

A measuring tape is useful for measuring longer lengths.

Yard stick

Yard sticks can be used for activities such as measuring the length of a room or a playing field. Demonstrate how to move one yard stick to measure a longer length or use several yard sticks to measure. You are not looking for accurate measuring at this stage, just the concept of using units to measure. Again, the metric system can be used at this stage.

Balance scale

A balance scale will help children to establish the idea of mass as a comparison. Use questions such as, "Which is lighter/heavier?" "How many cubes weigh the same as...?" Show children the weight measurements on packages of food and move on to using ounce or pound weights with a balance scale when they seem ready.

Geared clock

A geared clock is a useful tool becasue the hands turn around in relation to one another in the same way as on a real clock.

Play money

A set of plastic coins and bills is a useful resource for providing children with practice of handling money.